Teach Me...™

Japanese
and
More Japanese

by Judy Mahoney

Teach Me Japanese and More Japanese
Two books in one, twice the fun!
42 songs to sing and learn Japanese

The classic coloring books *Teach Me Japanese* and *Teach Me More Japanese* are now combined into a new bind up edition. This new edition includes the original coloring pages from both titles with a 60 minute audio CD. *Teach Me Japanese and More Japanese* also features six new pages of expanded vocabulary and activities.

Our mission at Teach Me Tapes is to enrich children through language learning. The *Teach Me...*series of books offers an engaging approach to language acquisition by using familiar children's songs and providing an audio to sing and learn. Studies show that a child's early exposure to new languages and cultures enhances learning skills and promotes a better appreciation of our multicultural world. We believe that it is important for children to listen, speak, read and write the language to enhance their learning experience. What better gift to offer our youth than the tools and ideas to understand the world we live in?

The Japanese language is unique in that it is made up of three writing systems. **Kanji,** or Chinese characters, was adopted into Japanese from Chinese, and served as the first written language in Japan. **Hiragana** is the phonetic writing system, designating the sound of each word. **Katakana** was the writing system developed to integrate foreign words into the Japanese language. In *Teach Me Japanese & More Japanese*, we introduce the **Hiragana** system with the emphasis on basic conversational language. We also use **rōmaji,** the Romanization of the Japanese sounds, to assist in the learning process.

Today's "global children" hold tomorrow's world in their hands!

Teach Me Japanese & More Japanese
Bind Up Edition
Book with CD
ISBN: 978-1-59972-604-5
Library of Congress Control Number: 2009901067

Copyright © 2009 Teach Me Tapes, Inc.
6016 Blue Circle Drive
Minnetonka, MN 55343-9104
www.teachmetapes.com
1-800-456-4656

Translations are not literal.
Printed in the United States of America
10 9 8 7 6 5 4 3 2

Teach me...
JAPANESE

A Musical Journey Through the Day

by
Judy Mahoney

Teach Me...™
www.teachmetapes.com

 Minna-de Utaeba

Minna-de utaeba utaeba utaeba
Minna-de utaeba tanoshiku narune
Anatamo watashimo minna tomodachi
Minna-de utaeba tanoshiku narune.

こんにちは。わたしの なまえは まり。
ko n ni chi wa. Wa ta shi no na ma e wa Mari.

あなたの なまえは なに。
A na ta no na ma e wa na ni.

わたしの かぞくを しょうかいします。
Wa ta shi no ka zo ku o shoo kai shimasu.

おとうさん
o to o sa n

おかあさん
o ka a sa n

わたし
wa ta shi

おとうと
o to o to

うちの ねこ
Uchi no ne ko

なまえは たま。
Na ma e wa Ta ma.
いろは はいいろ。
Iro wa hai iro.

うちの いぬ
Uchi no i nu

なまえは ポチ。
Na ma e wa Po chi.
いろは くろと しろ。
I ro wa kuro to shiro.

これは わたしの いえです。 やねは ちゃいろで
ko re wa watashi no i e desu. Yane wa chairo de
にわには きいろい はなが さいているの。
ni wa ni wa ki i ro i ha na ga sa i te i ru no.

わたしの へやの いろは あお。　もう ７じだわ。
Watashi no heya no iro wa ao.　Moo shichiji dawa.
さあ、おきましょう！おきましょう！
Saa, okimashoo.　Okimashoo.

 **Yaoya-san**

Yaoya-san-no omise-ni naranda
Shinamono mite goran
Yoku mite goran　kangaete goran
Tomato tomato.

 **Mada Neteruno**

Mada neteruno　mada neteruno
Onii-san, onii-san
Kyookai-no kane-ga natteiru-noni
Kin-kon-kan, kin-kon-kan.

4 YON

きょうは 月ようび。
kyo 。。 wa getsu yoobi.
ようびの なまえを しってる?
Yoo bi no namae o shitteru.

月ようび
Getsu yoo bi

火ようび
ka yoobi

水ようび
Sui yoobi

木ようび
Moku yoobi

金ようび
Kin yoobi

土ようび
Do yoo bi

日ようび
Nichi yoo bi

ようふくをきましょう。ブラウスをきて　ズボンと
Yoohuku o kimashoo. Burausu o kite　zu bo n to

くつを はいて
kutsu o hai te

ぼうしを かぶります。
boo shi o ka bu ri masu.

あさごはんを たべます。
A sa go ha n o ta be masu.
あさ ごはんは ごはんと
A sa go ha n wa go ha n to
みそしると めだまやき
mi so shi ru to me da ma ya ki
です。　おちゃも のみます。
de su.　O cha mo no mi masu.

🎵 **Atama Kata Hiza Ashi**

Atama kata hiza ashi hiza ashi
Atama kata hiza ashi hiza ashi
Me to mimi to kuchi to hana
Atama kata hiza ashi hiza ashi.

♪ **Ame Ame Itchae**

Ame ame itchae
Mata atode kiteyo
Ame ame itchae
Booya-ga sotode
Asobenai.

♪ **Niji**

Ao ya midori tottemo
Kiree-na iro
Pinku-ni murasaki kiiro
Niji-ni notte mitai.

©Teach Me Tapes, Inc. 1985

ここは わたしの がっこう。 まいあさ 「せんせい、おはよう
Ko ko wa wa ta shi no ga k ko o.　Ma i a sa "sen se e, o ha yo o
ございます」って あいさつします。
go za i ma su" tte　a i sa tsu shi ma su.
そして、 すうじと ひらがなの
So shi te,　suu ji to hi ra ga na no
おさらいをします。
o sa ra i o shi ma su.

一 二 三 四 五
六 七 八 九 十

あ	い	う	え	お
か	き	く	け	こ
さ	し	す	せ	そ
た	ち	つ	て	と
な	に	ぬ	ね	の
は	ひ	ふ	へ	ほ
ま	み	む	め	も
や	い	ゆ	え	よ
ら	り	る	れ	ろ
わ	い	う	え	を
ん				

AIUEO

A i u e o ka ki ku ke ko
Dareka-ga dokoka-de naratteru
Sa shi su se so ta chi tsu te to
Dareka-ga dokoka-de hanashiteru
Na ni nu ne no ha hi hu he ho
Dareka-ga dokoka-de wasureteru
Ma mi mu me mo ya i yu e yo
Dareka-ga dokoka-de utatteru
Ra ri ru re ro wa i u e o
Dareka-ga dokoka-de dokoka-de
Dareka-ga donatteru
N.

Merii-san no Hitsuji

Merii-san no hitsuji
Mee-mee hitsuji
Merii-san no hitsuji
Masshirone.

Doko-demo tsuiteiku
Mee-mee tsuiteiku
Doko-demo tsuiteiku
Kawaii-ne.

Ittoo-no Zoo-san

Ni-too-no zoo-san
Yatte-kita
Kumonosu-no ue-de
Asobooto
Tottemo tanoshi
Kattanode
Nakamao ittoo
Yobimashita.

(continue with)
3(San-too)
4(Yon-too)
5(Go-too)

Te-o Tatakimashoo

Te-o tatakimashoo
Tan-tan-tan, tan-tan-tan
Ashibumi shimashoo
Tan-tan-tan-tan, tan-tan-tan
Warai mashoo wa-ha-ha
Warai mashoo wa-ha-ha
Wa-ha-ha, wa-ha-ha, aa omoshiroi.

(repeat)
Okorimashoo un-un-un
Okorimashoo un-un-un
Un-un-un, un-un-un, aa omoshiroi.

(repeat)
Nakimashoo en-en-en
Nakimashoo en-en-en
En-en-en, en-en-en, aa omoshiroi.

♪ **Kuruma-no Taiya**

Kuruma-no taiya-wa kuru-kuru
Kuru-kuru, kuru-kuru
Kuruma-no taiya-wa kuru-kuru
Machi-no naka.

Kurakushon-wa bu-bu-bu
Bu-bu-bu, bu-bu-bu
Kurakushon-wa bu-bu-bu
Machi-no naka.

Kodomotachi-wa "Saa-tabeyoo"
"Hirugohan, saa-tabeyoo"
Kodomotachi-wa "Saa-tabeyoo"
Machi-no naka.

さあ、 ひるごはんです。 ひるごはんのあとは
Sa a hi ru go ha n de su. Hi ru go ha n no a to wa

おひるねします。
o hi ru ne shi ma su.

 Shizukani Me-o Tojite

Shizukani me-o tojite,
Papa-ga kanariya-o
Kattageyoo.

Utao wasureta torinaraba,
Daiya-no yubiwa-o
Kattageyoo.

Daiya-ga shinchuu-ni
Kawattara,
Kagami-o kattageyoo.

Kagami-ga kowaretemo,
Booya-wa ichiban kawaii ko.

12 JUU-NI

Abinyon-no Hashi-de

Hashi-no ue-de
Odoruyo odoruyo
Hashi-no ue-de
Wani-natte odoru.

Sakura Sakura

Sakura sakura noyamamo satomo
Miwatasu kagiri
Kasumi-ka kumo-ka asahi-ni niou
Sakura sakura hanazakari.

おひるねのあとは、こうえんへ
o hi ru ne no a to wa   ko o e n e
いきます。あひるがいるわね。
i ki ma su. A hi ru ga   i ru wa ne.
ともだちといっしょにはしの
to mo da chi to   i ssho ni   ha shi no
うえでうたったり、おどったり
u e de   u ta tta ri.   o do tta ri
するの。
su ru no.

Rokuwa-no Ahiru

Rokuwa-no ahiru-ga imashita, futotcho-ni yaseppochi iroiro
Demo haneno aru ahiru-ga, sentoo-ni-natte kwa-kwa-kwa
Kwa-kwa-kwa, kwa-kwa-kwa, sentoo-ni-natte kwa-kwa-kwa
Kwa-kwa-kwa, kwa-kwa-kwa.

おなかがすいたわね。そう、ばんごはんのじかんです。
O na ka ga su i ta wa ne. Soo ba n go ha n no ji ka n de su.

♪ Oo! Suzanna

Watasha Arabama kara Ruijiana-e
Banjoo-o motte dekaketa tokorodesu
Oo! Suzanna nakuno-janai
Banjoo-o motte dekaketa tokorodesu.

Ohoshi-sama

Ohoshi-sama hikaru
Ittai anata-wa daredeshoo
Osorano uede
Ohanashi shiteru
Ohoshisama hikaru
Ittai anata-wa daredeshoo.

Komori-Uta

Nen-nen kororiyo okororiyo
Booya-wa yoikoda nenneshina
Booya-no omori-wa doko-e itta
Ano yama koete sato-e itta
Satono miyage-ni nani moratta
Den-den-daiko ni shoo-no hue.

TRANSLATIONS

PAGE 1
The More We Get Together
The more we get together, together, together,
The more we get together the happier we'll be.
For your friends are my friends
And my friends are your friends
The more we get together the happier we'll be.

PAGE 2
Hello, my name is Mari. What is your name?
I will introduce my family: my mother, my father,
my younger brother and me.

PAGE 3
My cat. His name is Tama. His color is grey.
My dog. His name is Pochi. His color is black and
white. This is my house. The roof is brown
and in the garden yellow flowers bloom.

PAGE 4
The color of my room is blue. It is seven o'clock.
Now it's time to get up! Now it's time to get up!

The Vegetable Shop
Look at all the vegetables
Lined up at the vegetable shop.
Look at them carefully and think;
Tomato, tomato.
(Continue, repeating names of
other vegetables.)

Are You Sleeping
Are you sleeping, are you sleeping?
Brother John, Brother John?
Morning bells are ringing
Morning bells are ringing
Ding dang dong! Ding dang dong!

PAGE 5
Today is Monday. Do you know the
days of the week? Monday, Tuesday,
Wednesday, Thursday, Friday,
Saturday, Sunday.

PAGE 6
Let's get dressed. I put on my blouse,
my pants, my shoes and my hat.
For breakfast I eat rice, soup and fried
eggs. I drink tea, also.

PAGE 7
Head, Shoulders, Knees and Toes
Head and shoulders, knees and toes,
Knees and toes, *(repeat)*
Eyes and ears and mouth and nose
(Repeat first line)

PAGE 8
It is raining outside. I cannot go
for a walk today.

Rain, Rain, Go Away
Rain, rain, go away,
Come again another day,
Rain, rain, go away,
Little Johnny wants to play.

Rainbows
Sometimes blue and sometimes green
Prettiest colors I've ever seen
Pink and purple, yellow-whee!
I love to ride those rainbows.
©Teach Me Tapes, Inc. 1985

PAGE 9
Here is my school. Every morning I say
"Good morning, teacher." I review the
numbers and the alphabet.

The Alphabet Song
(The Japanese alphabet is woven into
these verses.)
Someone is learning somewhere
Someone is talking somewhere
Someone is forgetting somewhere
Someone is singing somewhere
Someone is yelling somewhere.

PAGE 10
Mary Had a Little Lamb
Mary had a little lamb
Its fleece was white as snow
Everywhere that Mary went
The lamb was sure to go.

One Elephant
One elephant went out to play
Upon a spider's web one day
He had such enormous fun that
He called for another elephant to come.

Let's Clap Hands
Let's clap hands, clap clap clap
Let's stamp feet, stamp stamp stamp.

Let's laugh, ha-ha-ha
Let's laugh, ha-ha-ha,
Ha-ha-ha, ha-ha-ha,
Oh it's fun!

Let's get angry, unh-unh-unh
Let's get angry, unh-unh-unh,
Unh-unh-unh, unh-unh-unh,
Oh it's fun!

Let's cry, wah-wah-wah
Let's cry wah-wah-wah,
Wah-wah-wah, wah-wah-wah,
Oh it's fun!

TRANSLATIONS

PAGE 11
After school, we go home by car.

The Wheels on the Car
The wheels on the car go round and round,
Round and round, round and round,
The wheels on the car go round and round
All around the town.

The horn on the car goes beep beep beep,
Beep beep beep, beep beep beep,
The horn on the car goes beep beep beep,
All around the town.

The children in the car go, "Let's have lunch,"
"Let's have lunch," "Let's have lunch,"
The children in the car go, "Let's have lunch,"
All around the town.

Lunch Dialogue
Mother: Lunch is ready.
Children: What's for lunch?
Mother: Kitsune-udon. (Noodles)
Everyone: Itadakimasu. (Greeting
* before eating.)*
Mother: Be careful. It's hot.
Children: Delicious!
Mother: What did you do at school?
Mari: I made cranes with paper.
Mother: Did you do a good job?
Mari: Yes. I made them in red
* and green.*
Younger brother: I flew a kite.
* It went up very high.*
Mother: Really! That's great.

PAGE 12
It is lunch time. After lunch we take a nap.

Hush Little Baby
Hush little baby don't say a word
Papa's going to buy you a mockingbird
If that mockingbird don't sing
Papa's going to buy you a diamond ring
If that diamond ring turns brass
Papa's going to buy you a looking glass
If that looking glass falls down
You'll still be the sweetest little baby in town.

PAGE 13
After our naps, we go to the park. I see
the ducks. I sing and dance with my
friends on the bridge.

On the Bridge of Avignon
On the bridge of Avignon
They're all dancing, they're all dancing
On the bridge of Avignon
They're all dancing round and round.

The Cherry Blossom Song
Cherry blossoms, cherry blossoms
On mountains, in villages
As far as you can see.
They look like fog or clouds
They are fragrant in the morning sun.
Cherry blossoms, cherry blossoms
In full bloom.

Six Little Ducks
Six little ducks that I once knew,
Fat ones, skinny ones, fair ones too,
But the one little duck
With the feather on his back,
He led the others with his
Quack, quack, quack,
Quack, quack, quack,
Quack, quack, quack,
He led the others with his
Quack, quack, quack.

PAGE 14
I am hungry. It is dinner time.

Oh, Susanna
Well I come from Alabama
With my banjo on my knee
Going to Louisiana, my true love for to see.
Oh, Susanna, don't you cry for me
'Cause I come from Alabama
With my banjo on my knee.

PAGE 15
It's night time. Can you see the stars
in the sky? Goodnight, mother. Good-
night, father. Goodnight, everyone.
Goodnight.

Twinkle, Twinkle
Twinkle, twinkle little star
How I wonder what you are
Up above the world so high
Like a diamond in the sky
Twinkle, twinkle little star
How I wonder what you are.

Lullabye Song
Night, night baby go to sleep
You are a good baby
Go to sleep
Where did your babysitter go?
She went home to the other side
Of the mountain.
What did she bring you?
She brought a little rattle-drum
And a flute.

Goodnight My Friends, Goodnight.

Note: Translations are not always literal.

From page 9:

The Japanese alphabet has 46 characters.

a	i	u	e	o
ka	ki	ku	ke	ko
sa	shi	su	se	so
ta	chi	tsu	te	to
na	ni	nu	ne	no
ha	hi	hu	he	ho
ma	mi	mu	me	mo
ya	i	yu	e	yo
ra	ri	ru	re	ro
wa	i	u	e	o
N				

Pronunciation

Use this guide to help pronounce a word correctly.

Letter	Pronounced	Letter	Pronounced
a	as "a" in ah	g	as "g" in go
e	as "e" in bed	ei	as "ay" in say
i	as "ee" in feet	ai	as "y" in sky
o	as "o" in no	oy	as "oy" in toy
u	as "oo" in zoo		

Greetings

There are special greetings for different times of the day and different ways to say the greeting depending on who you are talking to.

Ohayou Gozaimasu = Good Morning (formal)

   Or just use **Ohayou** for friends and coworkers

Konichiwa = Hello (basic all around day time greeting)

   Domo = hello for very familiar people

Konban Wa = Good Evening

Moshi Moshi = Hello (greeting for on the phone or entering a room)

O Genki Desu Ka? = How are you?

   The most common answer is **"Hai, Genki Desu"** meaning "I am fine"

Hajimemashite = Nice to meet you (for the first time you meet)

Sayanara = Goodbye

Common Phrases

Sumimasen = Excuse me

Gomen Nasai = Pardon me or I am sorry

Arigatou = Thank you

Arigatou Gozaimasu = Formal thank you, but most commonly used

Tondemonai = You are welcome

Dozo = Please

Kudasai = Another word for please

Hai = Yes

Iie = No

Nanji desu ka? = What time is it?

Toire wa doko ni arimasu ka? = Where is the toilet?

Teach me more... JAPANESE

by
Judy Mahoney

A Musical Journey Through the Year

Learn Japanese the fun way!

Teach Me™
www.teachmetapes.com

まり：こんにちは。わたしのなまえは まりです。うちには いぬが います。いぬのなまえは ポチ。うちには ねこも います。ねこのなまえは たま。トム：こんにちは。ぼくは ともだちのトムです。さあ、ぼくたちと いっしょに いちねんを すごしましょう。

Anata-ga Utaeba

Anata-ga utaeba, watashi-mo utau, minna-de utaoo, utaeba tanoshi.
Anata-ga utaeba, watashi-mo utau, atsusa-mo wasure, samusa-mo hukitobu.

トム： はる。 ぼくは にわに はなの たねを まきます。 ぼくの
To mu: Ha ru. Bo ku wa ni wa ni ha na no ta ne o ma ki ma su. Bo ku no
そだてた あかときいろの バラの はなを みて。 きれいでしょう。
so da te ta a ka to ki i ro no ba ra no ha na o mi te. Ki re e de sho o.
まり： わたしは にわに やさいの たねを まきます。 ことしは トマト
Ma ri: Wa ta shi wa ni wa ni ya sa i no ta ne o ma ki ma su. Ko to shi wa to ma to
と ピーマンと にんじんを そだてるの。
to pi i man to ni n ji n o so da te ru no.

Mugi-wa Dokokara

Mugi-wa dokokara
Mugi-wa dokokara
Doko-kara kurunoka
Dareka oshiete.

Nooka-no ojisan
Tane-o makimasu
Soko-kara me-ga dete
Sodatte yukuno.

Haru-ga Kita

Haru-ga kita; haru-ga kita;
Doko-ni kita. Yama-ni kita;
Sato-ni kita; no-nimo kita.

Hana-ga saku; hana-ga saku;
Doko-ni saku. Yama-ni saku;
Sato-ni saku; no-nimo saku.

Tori-ga naku; tori-ga naku;
Doko-de naku. Yama-de naku;
Sato-de naku; no-demo naku.

Doobutsuen-e Ikooyo

Doobutsuen-e ikooyo, doobutsuen-e ikooyo
Doobutsuen-wa zuuttenda, ureshiina.

* *Saa ikooyo zuu, zuu, zuu*
  Kimi-mo yuu, yuu, yuu
  Minna-de goo, goo, goo
  Saa ikooyo zuu, zuu, zuu.

Osaru-san-wa kinobori, joozusa, joozusa
Buranko yura yura, tanoshiina.
  *Repeat ***

Wani-san-wa sui sui,
Oyoguyo mizu-no-naka
Sui sui oyoguyo, iikimochi.
  *Repeat ***

まり： きょう わたしたちは どうぶつえんへ いきます。 ほら、ライオンと キリンと サルが いるわよ。
Ma ri: Kyo o wa ta shi ta chi wa do o bu tsu e n e i ki ma su. Ho ra, ra i o n to ki ri n to sa ru ga i ru wa yo.

トム： ぼくの いちばんすきな どうぶつは ワニ。
To mu: Bo ku no i chi ba n su ki na do o bu tsu wa wa ni.

Tingaleyo

Tingaleyo oideyo roba
Tingaleyo oideyo roba
Boku-no roba-wa hayai toki-mo-aru
Boku-no roba-wa noroi toki-mo-aru.

まり： わたしのたんじょうびは 5がつ10か。ともだちを
Mari: Watashi no tanjoobi wa Gogatsu tooka. Tomodachi o
よんで パーティーをします。おかあさんがまるいおおきな
yonde paatii o shimasu. Okaasan ga marui ookina
ケーキを やいてくれるの。
keeki o yaite kureru no.
トム： さあ、「せんちょうさんのめいれい」のゲームをしようよ。
Tomu: Saa, "Senchoo-san-no meeree." no geemu o shiyoo yo.

♪ **Tanjoobi** Kyoo-wa tanjoobi Mari-chan-no tanjoobi Tanjoobi omedetoo Tanoshii tanjoobi.	**Senchoo-san-no Meeree** "Senchoo-san-no meeree": …"Migite-o atama-ni nosete." …"Jimen-ni te-o tsuite." …"Aruite." …"Te-o tataite." …"Jibun-no namae-o itte." "Ookina koe-de waratte": "Senchoo-san-wa meereeshinakatta-yo."

トム： はるのあとには なつが きます。 ぼくたちは なつにうみ
To mu: Ha ru no a to ni wa na tsu ga ki ma su. Bo ku ta chi wa na tsu ni u mi
へ いきます。 ぼくは ビーチボール
e i ki ma su. Bo ku wa bi i chi bo o ru
と おもちゃの ふねを もっていくよ。
to o mo cha no hu ne o mo tte i ku yo.
まり： わたしは バケツと シャベル
Ma ri: wa ta shi wa ba ke tsu to sha be ru
を もっていくわ。
o mo tte i ku wa.
まり： みずぎを きて おおきな すな
Ma ri: Mi zu gi o ki te o o ki na su na
の おしろを つくっているの。
no o shi ro o tsu ku tte i ru no.
トム： あっ。 ポチ、 こわしちゃ だめ。
To mu: A, Po chi, ko wa shi cha da me.

Seeringu

Seeringu, seeringu umi-no ue
Jakku-ga ie-ni kaeru-made
Arashi-ni takusan audeshoo
Tsuyoi kaze takusan hukudeshoo.

Koge Koge Booto

Koge koge booto
Yuruyakani
Yura, yura, yura, yura
Yume-no naka.

Umi

Umi-wa hiroina ookiina
Tsuki-ga noborushi, higa shizumu.

Umi-wa oonami aoi nami
Yurete doko-made tsuzukuyara.

Umi-ni ohune-o ukabashite
Ittemitai-na yoso-no kuni.

まり： ああ、おなかがすいた。おべんとうをたべましょう。
Ma ri: A a, o na ka ga su i ta. O be n to o o ta be ma sho o.

おべんとうは おにぎりとゆでたまご。バナナもあるわ。
O be n to o wa o ni gi ri to yu de ta ma go. Ba na na mo a ru wa.

トム： おいしい。やだな、このありみてよ。
To mu: O i shi i. Ya da na, ko no a ri mi te yo.

まり： おべんとうをたべおわったら、さんぽにいこうね。
Mari: O be n to o o ta be o wa tta ra, san po ni i ko o ne.

♪ **Banana Booto Songu**

De-o-mise-de-o yoake mae-ni bananagari *(repeat)*
Banana-o takusan totte, yoake-nya ie-e kaeru
Banana-o takusan tsumiage, yoake-nya ie-e kaeru
Goshujin banana-o kazoetekure, yoake-nya ie-e kaeru *(repeat)*
Roku-husa, nana-husa, hachi-husa, yoake-nya ie-e kaeru *(repeat)*
Kireena umasoona banana, yoake-nya ie-e kaeru *(repeat)*

まり：わたしたちは きょう はくぶつかんへ いきます。
Mari: Wa ta shi ta chi wa kyo o ha ku bu tsu ka n e i ki ma su.

トム：たくさん きょうりゅうが いるから、ぼく はくぶつかんが
To mu: Ta ku sa n kyo o ryu u ga i ru ka ra, bo ku ha ku bu tsu ka n ga

だいすきなんだ。トリケラトップスが いるよ。あたまに みっつ
da i su ki na n da. To ri ke ra to p pu su ga i ru yo. A ta ma ni mi t tsu

もつのが ある。
mo tsu no ga a ru.

7 NANA

まり: つぎは となりの びじゅつ
Ma ri: Tsu gi wa to na ri no bi ju tsu
かんへ いきます。
ka n e i ki ma su.
トム: ぼくは ゴヤの うしの え
To mu: Bo ku wa Go ya no u shi no e
が すきなんだ。 とうぎゅうしに
ga su ki na n da. To o gyu u shi ni
なってみたいな。
na t te mi ta i na.
まり: ねえ。 ゴッホの えを みて。
Ma ri: Ne e. Go h ho no e o mi te.
この ひまわりは うちの にわの
Ko no hi ma wa ri wa u chi no ni wa no
と そっくりよ。
to so k ku ri yo.

Marui Wa-no Naka

Marui wa-no naka ra ra ra ra ra
Tottemo genkina kawaii ko
Mauri wa-no naka ra ra ra ra ra
Ohisama-to nakayoshi run run run.

2. Ugoite misete...
3. Umi-o sukippu...
4. Odotte misete...

8 HACHI

まり: なつのあとには あきがきます。 きのはのいろが あかやきいろに
Mari: Na tsu no a to ni wa a ki ga ki ma su. Ki no ha no i ro ga a ka ya ki i ro ni
かわってとってもきれい。 わたしはおちばやどんぐりをあつめています。
ka wa tte to tte mo ki re e. Wa ta shi wa o chi ba ya do n gu ri o a tsu me te i ma su.
あっ、むしのこえ...
A, mu shi no ko e...

Mushi-no Koe

Are matsumushi-ga naite iru
Chinchiro chinchiro chinchirorin
Are suzumushi-mo nakidashita
Rin rin rin rin riin rin
Aki-no yonaga-o nakitoosu
Aa omoshiroi mushi-no koe.

Donguri Koro Koro

Donguri koro koro donburiko
Oike-ni hamatte saa taihen
Dojoo-ga detekite konnichiwa
Botchan issho-ni asobimashoo.

Additional verses on page 16

トム： きょう ぼくたちは まりちゃんのおじいちゃんのまきばへ
To mu: Kyo o bo ku ta chi wa Ma ri cha n no o ji i cha n no ma ki ba e
あそびにいきます。 うしやにわ
a so bi ni i ki ma su. U shi ya ni wa
とりやぶたにえさをやりたいな。
to ri ya bu ta ni e sa o ya ri ta i na.
まり： おじいちゃんは いま ひつじ
Ma ri: O ji i cha n wa i ma hi tsu ji
のけをかっています。 そのあと
no ke o ka t te i ma su. So no a to
おじいちゃんが トラクターで わた
o ji i cha n ga to ra ku ta a de wa ta
したちをドライブにつれていって
shi ta chi o do ra i bu ni tsu re te i t te
くれるの。ほしくさのクッションが
ku re ru no. Ho shi ku sa no ku s sho n ga
きもちいいわ。
ki mo chi i i wa.

Mee Mee Hitsuji

Mee mee hitsuji kegawa aru
Hai hai mihukuro gozaimasu
Goshujin-ni hitotsu gohujin-nimo
Soshite saigo-wa booya-ni
Mee mee hitsuji kegawa aru
Hai hai mihukuro gozaimasu.

Ojiichan-no Makiba

Saa minna-de ikooyo, ojiichan-no makiba-e
Minna-de tanoshiku, ojiichan-no makiba-e.

Makiba-niwa ushi-ga irunosa
Ookina chairoi ushi-ga
Ushi-wa koo nakunosa (Moo)

Makiba-niwa mendori-mo iruyo
Akakute chiisai mendori
Sore-wa koo nakunosa (Kokekokkoo)

Makudonarudo Jiisan

Makudonarudo jiisan katteiru
Koushi-o takusan katteiru
Hora moo moo moo, moo moo moo
Atchi-mo kotchi-mo doko-demo moo, moo
Makudonarudo jiisan katteiru.

Niwatori..."kokekokkoo"
Koneko..."nyaa nyaa nyaa"
Hitsuji..."mee mee mee"

まり： きょうは わたしの がっこうの うんどうかい。 あかと しろの チー
Mari: Kyo o wa wa ta shi no ga k ko o no u n do o ka i. A ka to shi ro no chi i

ムに わかれて、 かけっこや たまいれを するの。
mu ni wa ka re te, ka ke k ko ya ta ma i re o su ru no.

トム： ぼくは つなひきと パンくいきょうそうが すきさ。
To mu: Bo ku wa tsu na hi ki to pa n ku i kyo o so o ga su ki sa.

まり： おとうさんや おかあさん、それに せんせいたちも はしるのよ。
Mari: O to o sa n ya o ka a sa n, so re ni se n se e ta chi mo ha shi ru no yo.

うんどうかいは わたしの いちばんすきな がっこうぎょうじです。
U n do o ka i wa wa ta shi no i chi ba n su ki na ga k ko o gyo o ji de su.

トム：アメリカにすんでいるいとこからてがみがとどきました。
To mu: A me ri ka ni sun de i ru i to ko ka ra te ga mi ga to do ki ma shi ta.

アメリカでは ハロウィーンというおまつりがあって、オレンジいろ
A me ri ka de wa Ha ro wi i n to i u o ma tsu ri ga a tte, o ren ji i ro

のおおきなかぼちゃをくりぬいて ランタンをつくります。まり：
no o o ki na ka bo cha o ku ri nu i te ran ta n o tsu ku ri ma su. Ma ri:

わたしたちは トムくんのいとこがおくってくれた ハロウィーンの
Wa ta shi ta chi wa To mu ku n no i to ko ga o ku tte ku re ta Ha ro wi i n no

いしょうをきてみました。 わたしは あかずきん、トムくんは
i sho o o ki te mi ma shi ta. Wa ta shi wa a ka zu ki n, To mu ku n wa

カーボーイに なりました。 ポチはおおかみです。アメリカのこど
ka a bo o i ni na ri ma shi ta. Po chi wa o o ka mi de su. A me ri ka no ko do

もたちは きんじょをまわって おかしをもらうそうです。たのしそ
mo ta chi wa ki n jo o ma wa tte o ka shi o mo ra u so o de su. Ta no shi so

うね。トム：ハロウィーンがおわると、１１がつになります。
o ne. To mu: Ha ro wi i n ga o wa ru to, juu-ichi ga tsu ni na ri ma su.

Itsutsu-no Kabocha

Itsutsu-no kabocha-ga suwatteta. Hitotsu-me itta, "Moo osoi."
Hutatsu-me itta, "Majo iruyo." Mittsu-me itta, "Shirumonka."
Yottsu-me itta, "Nigeyooyo." Itsutsu-me itta, "Boku wakuwaku."
Hyuutto kaze huki akari kie, itsutsu-no kabocha-wa kietatosa.

トム： みて。 ゆきが ふってきた。 そとへでて ゆきで あそぼう。
To mu: Mi te. Yu ki ga hu t te ki ta. So to e de te yu ki de a so bo o.
ぼくたちは ソリすべりをします。 まり： それからゆきだるまをつく
Bo ku ta chi wa so ri su be ri o shi ma su. Ma ri: So re ka ra yu ki da ru ma o tsu ku
ります。 すみのめと にんじんの
ri ma su. Su mi no me to nin ji n no
はなをつけて。 やまたかぼうを
ha na o tsu ke te, ya ma ta ka bo o o
かぶせます。 おかあさんの
ka bu se ma su. O ka a sa n no
えりまきもしてあげました。
e ri ma ki mo shi te a ge ma shi ta.

Yukidaruma-no Uta

Yamatakaboo-o
Ikini kabutta
Watashi-no tomodachi
Daredeshoo.

Me-wa kuroku
Hana-wa ninjin
Ude-wa eda-no
Shiroi hito.

Huyu-shika aenai
Sono-hito-no namae
Atete goranyo
Daredeshoo.

Kiyoshi Kono-Yoru

Kiyoshi kono-yoru
Hoshi-wa hikari
Sukui-no miko-wa
Mihaha-no mune-ni
Nemuritamoo
Yume yasuku.

１月

あけまして おめでとう

まり： おしょうがつは いちねんでいち
Mari: O sho o ga tsu wa i chi ne n de i chi
ばん おおきな ぎょうじです。 おしょう
ba n o o ki na gyo o ji de su. O sho o
がつには かどまつをたてたり、もち
ga tsu ni wa ka do ma tsu o ta te ta ri, mo chi
つきをしたりします。 こどもたちは
tsu ki o shi ta ri shi ma su. Ko do mo ta chi wa
おとしだまをもらいます。
o to shi da ma o mo ra i ma su.
トム： おおみそかには じょやのか
Tomu: O o mi so ka ni wa jo ya no ka
ねをきいて、 としこしそばをたべま
ne o ki i te, to shi ko shi so ba o ta be ma
す。そして しんねんには じんじゃに
su. So shi te shi n ne n ni wa ji n ja ni
はつもうでにいきます。
ha tsu mo o de ni i ki ma su.

Oshoogatsu

Moo ikutsu neruto oshoogatsu
Oshoogatsu-niwa tako agete
Koma-o mawashite asobimashoo
Hayaku koi koi oshoogatsu.

Moo ikutsu neruto oshoogatsu
Oshoogatsu-niwa mari tsuite
Oibane tsuite asobimashoo
Hayaku koi koi oshoogatsu.

Mame Maki

Oni-wa soto. Huku-wa uchi. Para para para para mame-no oto.
Oni-wa kossori nigete yuku.

Oni-wa soto. Huku-wa uchi. Para para para para mame-no oto.
Hayaku ohairi huku-no-kami.

まり：２がつには せつぶんが あります。いえのなかのあく
Mari: Ni ga tsu ni wa se tsu bu n ga a ri ma su. I e no na ka no a ku

をおいはらって あたらしいはるが むかえられるように まめ
o o i ha ra tte a ta ra shi i ha ru ga mu ka e ra re ru yo o ni ma me

まきをします。
ma ki o shi ma su.

トム：おにのおめんをつけたひとに まめをぶつけて、いえ
To mu: o ni no o me n o tsu ke ta hi to ni ma me o bu tsu ke te, i e

からおいだします。まいたまめを としのかずだけ ひろって
ka ra o i da shi ma su. Ma i ta ma me o to shi no ka zu da ke hi ro tte

たべるといいって まりちゃんのおばあちゃんが いってたよ。
ta be ru to i i tte Ma ri cha n no o ba a cha n ga i tte ta yo.

まりとトム：おにはそと、ふくはうち。おにはそと、ふく
Mari to Tomu: O ni wa so to, Hu ku wa u chi. O ni wa so to, Hu ku

はうち。
wa u chi.

まり：これで いちねんの つきの よびかたが わかりましたね。
Mari: Ko re de i chi ne n no tsu ki no yo bi ka ta ga wa ka ri ma shi ta ne.

もういちど いっしょにいってみましょう。１がつ。２がつ。
Mo o i chi do i ssho ni i tte mi ma sho o. Ichi ga tsu, Ni ga tsu,

３がつ。４がつ、５がつ。６がつ。７がつ。８がつ。９がつ。
San ga tsu, Shi ga tsu, Go ga tsu, Roku ga tsu, Shichi ga tsu, Hachi ga tsu, Ku ga tsu,

10がつ。11がつ。12がつ。
Juu ga tsu, Juu-ichi ga tsu, Juu-ni ga tsu.

まりとトム：さようなら。
Mari to Tomu: Sa yo o na ra.

１月、２月、３月、４月、５月、６月、７月、８月、９月、10月、
Ichi gatsu, Ni gatsu, San gatsu, Shi gatsu, Go gatsu, Roku gatsu, Shichi gatsu, Hachi gatsu, Ku gatsu, Juu gatsu,

11月、12月。さようなら。またあいましょう。
Juu-ichi gatsu, Juu-ni gatsu. Sa yo o na ra. Ma ta a i ma sho o.

Donguri Koro Koro
Additional Verses from Page 9

Donguri koro koro yorokonde
Shibaraku issho-ni asonda-ga
Yappari oyama-ga koishii-to
Naite-wa dojoo-o komaraseta.

Donguri koro koro naiteruto
Usagi-ga dete kite dooshitano
Sorenara watashi-ga ouchi-made
Okutte itte agemashoo.

The Japanese hiragana alphabet
has 46 characters:

a	i	u	e	o
ka	ki	ku	ke	ko
sa	shi	su	se	so
ta	chi	tsu	te	to
na	ni	nu	ne	no
ha	hi	hu	he	ho
ma	mi	mu	me	mo
ya	i	yu	e	yo
ra	ri	ru	re	ro
wa	i	u	e	o
n				

あ	い	う	え	お
か	き	く	け	こ
さ	し	す	せ	そ
た	ち	つ	て	と
な	に	ぬ	ね	の
は	ひ	ふ	へ	ほ
ま	み	む	め	も
や	い	ゆ	え	よ
ら	り	る	れ	ろ
わ	い	う	え	を
ん				

NOTES

TRANSLATIONS

PAGE 1
You'll Sing a Song
You'll sing a song and I'll sing a song
And we'll sing a song together.
It's fun when we sing together.
You'll sing a song and I'll sing a song
We forget the hot and cold weather.

MARI: Hello. My name is Mari. There's a dog at our home. The dog's name is Pochi. There's a cat at our home, too. The cat's name is Tama.
TOM: Hello. I'm Tom, Mari's friend. Let's spend the year together.

PAGE 2 MARCH
TOM: (It is) Spring. I plant flower seeds in the garden. Look at the red and yellow roses I grew. Aren't they pretty?
MARI: I plant vegetable seeds in the garden. This year I will grow tomatoes, peppers and carrots.

Oats and Beans and Barley
Where does wheat come from? (*Repeat*)
Someone please tell me where it comes from.

A farmer plants a seed.
A sprout comes out and it grows.

Haru-ga Kita (Spring Song)
Spring has come; spring has come.
Where has it come? It has come to
The mountains, villages and fields.

Flowers bloom; flowers bloom.
Where do they bloom? They bloom in
The mountains, villages and fields.

Birds sing; birds sing.
Where do they sing? They sing in
The mountains, villages and fields.

PAGE 3 APRIL
MARI: Today we are going to the zoo. Look, there are the lions, giraffes and monkeys.
TOM: My favorite animal is the crocodile.

Going to the Zoo
Let's go to the zoo. Let's go to the zoo.
A zoo is called "Zoo" (in English).
I'm happy.

Let's go to the zoo, zoo, zoo.
You (are going) too, you, you, you.
All together go, go, go.
Let's go to the zoo, zoo, zoo.

Monkeys are good at climbing.
They are swinging. It is fun.

Crocodiles swim in the water.
They swim easily. It feels good.

Tingalayo
Tingalayo, come on donkey. (*Repeat*)
My donkey is sometimes fast.
My donkey is sometimes slow.

PAGE 4 MAY
Happy Birthday
Today is a birthday,
Mari's birthday.
Happy birthday,
Joyful birthday.

MARI: My birthday is May 10. I'll invite my friends and have a party. (My) mother will bake me a big, round cake.
TOM: OK, let's play "Command of the Captain." (Simon Says)

Simon Says Game
Captain's command ..."put your right hand on your head"
..."touch the ground"
..."walk"
..."clap your hands"
..."say your name"
"Laugh out loud." "Captain didn't command!"

PAGE 5 JUNE
TOM: After spring, comes summer. We go to the beach in summer. I bring my beachball and toy boat.
MARI: I bring my pail and shovel. We put on our swimsuits and we are making a big sand castle.
TOM: Oh! Pochi, don't knock it down!

Row, Row, Row
Row, row, boat,
Gently.
Rocking, rocking, rocking, rocking
(As) in a dream.

Sailing, Sailing
Sailing, sailing on the ocean
Until Jack comes home.
He'll meet a lot of stormy weather
A lot of strong wind will blow.

Umi (Ocean Song)
The ocean is wide and big.
The moon rises and the sun sets.

The ocean has big waves, blue waves.
I wonder how far they go.

Launch the boat into the ocean.
I want to go to other countries.

PAGE 6 JULY
MARI: Oh, I'm hungry. Let's eat lunch. Lunch is rice balls and boiled eggs. There are bananas, too.
TOM: It is delicious. Oh, no! Look at this ant.
MARI: After we finish eating lunch, let's go for a walk.

Day-O
Day-O, I pick bananas before dawn.
I pick a lot of bananas and go home at dawn.
I pile up a lot of bananas and go home at dawn.
Count the bananas, master, I go home at dawn.
Six bunch, seven bunch, eight bunch.
I go home at dawn.
Day-O, I pick bananas before dawn.
Beautiful and delicious-looking bananas.
I go home at dawn.
Six bunch, seven bunch, eight bunch.
I go home at dawn.
Day-O, I pick bananas before dawn.
Count the bananas, master,
I go home at dawn.

PAGE 7 AUGUST
MARI: Today we are going to the museum.
TOM: I like the museum very much because there are many dinosaurs. Look, there is a triceratops. It has three points on its head.

PAGE 8 AUGUST
MARI: Next we go to the art museum next door.
TOM: I like the painting of bulls by Goya. I want to be a matador.
MARI: Look at the painting by Van Gogh. These sunflowers look like the ones in our garden.

Brown Girl in the Ring
In the ring, la, la, la, la, la
Very energetic and cute girl
In the ring, la, la, la, la, la
She's friendly with the sun.

2. Show me a motion...
3. Skip across the ocean...
4. Show me dancing...

PAGE 9 SEPTEMBER
MARI: After summer, autumn comes. The color of leaves on the trees turn red and yellow and they look very pretty.
I'm gathering fallen leaves and acorns. I hear the chirping of the insects...

Mushi-no Koe (Cricket Song)
Listen, Matsumushi (a cricket) is chirping.
(Sound-chinchiro)
Listen, Suzumushi (another cricket)
Started chirping, too.
(Sound-rin)
Through the long nights of autumn.
It is fun listening to insects chirp.

Donguri Koro Koro (Acorn Song)
Acorn rolled and rolled
And fell into a pond.

Loach* came out and said, "Hello,"
Play with me, little boy.
Eel-like snake
Acorn was happy
And played with Loach for a while
But he missed the mountain.
He cried and gave Loach a hard time.

When Acorn was crying
Rabbit came and asked him:
"What's the matter?"
And said, "I'll take you home."

PAGE 10 OCTOBER
TOM: Today we'll visit Mari's grandpa's farm. I want to feed the cows, chickens and pigs.
MARI: Grandpa is now shearing the wool from the sheep. Later he's going to take us for a ride in his tractor. The cushion of hay feels good.

Down on Grandpa's Farm
Now, let's go together to Grandpa's farm.
Joyfully together to Grandpa's farm.

There are cows at the farm.
Big brown cows.
The cow makes a sound like this, "Moo —" (*Repeat*)

There are also hens at the farm.
Red little hens.
The hen makes a sound like this, "Kokekokkoo" (*Repeat*)

Baa Baa Black Sheep
Baa, baa sheep. Have you any wool?
Yes, yes, there are three bags.
One bag for my master and one for the lady, too.
And the last one is for the little boy.
Baa, baa sheep. Have you any wool?
Yes, yes there are three bags.

Old MacDonald
Old MacDonald has (on his farm)
He has many calves which go moo, moo, moo
There, here and everywhere, moo, moo
Old MacDonald has (on his farm).

Old MacDonald has (on his farm)
He has many chickens, which go kokekokkoo
There, here and everywhere, kokko
Old MacDonald has (on his farm).

Old MacDonald has (on his farm)
He has many kittens, which go nyaa, nyaa, nyaa
There, here and everywhere, nyaa, nyaa
Old MacDonald has (on his farm).

Old MacDonald has (on his farm)
He has many sheep, which go mee, mee, mee
There, here and everywhere, mee, mee
Old MacDonald has (on his farm).

PAGE 11 OCTOBER

MARI: It is field day at my school today. We are divided into a red team and a white team and we run and play tamaire. (Tamaire is a game which involves throwing as many bean bags as possible into a basket.)
TOM: I like tug-of-war and the bread-eating race.
MARI: Fathers, mothers and the teachers run, too. The field day is my favorite school event.

PAGE 12 OCTOBER/NOVEMBER

TOM: A letter came from a cousin who lives in the U.S. In the U.S. they have a holiday called Halloween and they carve a big orange pumpkin to make a lantern.
MARI: We put on the Halloween costumes Tom's cousin sent. I become Little Red Riding Hood and Tom becomes a cowboy. Pochi was a wolf. I heard that American children go around the neighborhood and get candy. It sounds like fun.
TOM: After Halloween, it is November.

Five Little Pumpkins

Five little pumpkins sitting on a gate
First one said,"Oh my it's getting late."
Second one said, "There are witches in the air."
The third one said,"But we don't care."
The fourth one said,"Let's run and run and run."
The fifth one said, "I'm ready for some fun."
"Oo-oo," went the wind and out went the light
And the five little pumpkins rolled out of sight.

PAGE 13 DECEMBER

TOM: Look, snow is falling. Let's go outside and play in the snow. We go sledding.
MARI: Then we build a snowman. We put on coal eyes, a carrot nose and a derby hat. We also put on (my) mother's scarf.

Snowman Rock 'n Roll

Who's my friend
Who wears a cool derby hat?

He is a snowy person with black eyes,
A carrot nose and stick arms.

Guess the name of the person you can meet
Only in winter.
Who is he?

Silent Night

Holy tonight
Stars shine
The Savior child
Is in the arms of his mother
He's sleeping
Sweet dreams.

PAGE 14 JANUARY

MARI: The New Year is the biggest event of the year. In the New Year, we put up kadomatsu (pine ornaments) and make rice cakes. Children receive New Year's allowances.
TOM: On New Year's Eve, we hear temple bells and eat buckwheat noodles (Toshikoshi-soba, special New Year's Eve noodles). And on New Year's Day, we go to a shrine to make a wish.

New Year Song

How many nights do I have to sleep until
The New Year?
In the New Year, let's play
Flying a kite and spinning a top
Come New Year, come quickly.

How many nights do I have to sleep until
The New Year?
In the New Year, let's play
Bouncing a ball and hanetsuki*
Come New Year, come quickly.
*Japanese game like badminton

PAGE 16 FEBRUARY

MARI: In February we have Setsubun (the beginning of spring). We throw beans to drive out evil from the house and to welcome a new spring.
TOM: We throw beans at the person wearing a demon mask and drive him out of the house. Mari's grandma said that we should pick up the same number of beans as our age and eat them.
MARI & TOM: Out demons; in good fortune. Out demons; in good fortune.

Bean Song

Out demons. In good fortune.
Patter, patter, patter, patter.
We hear the sound of beans
Demons sneak out of the house.

Out demons. In good fortune.
Patter, patter, patter, patter.
We hear the sound of beans
God of wealth, come in quickly.

MARI: Now we know the months of the year, don't we? Let's say them one more time all together. JANUARY, FEBRUARY, MARCH APRIL, MAY, JUNE, JULY, AUGUST, SEPTEMBER, OCTOBER, NOVEMBER, DECEMBER.
MARI & TOM: Goodbye!

Months of the Year Song (LaBamba)

January, February, March, April, May, June, July, August, September, October, November, December.
Goodbye! I'll see you.

Note: All efforts have been made to include literal translations.

Teach Me...
LEARNING LANGUAGE THROUGH SONGS AND STORIES

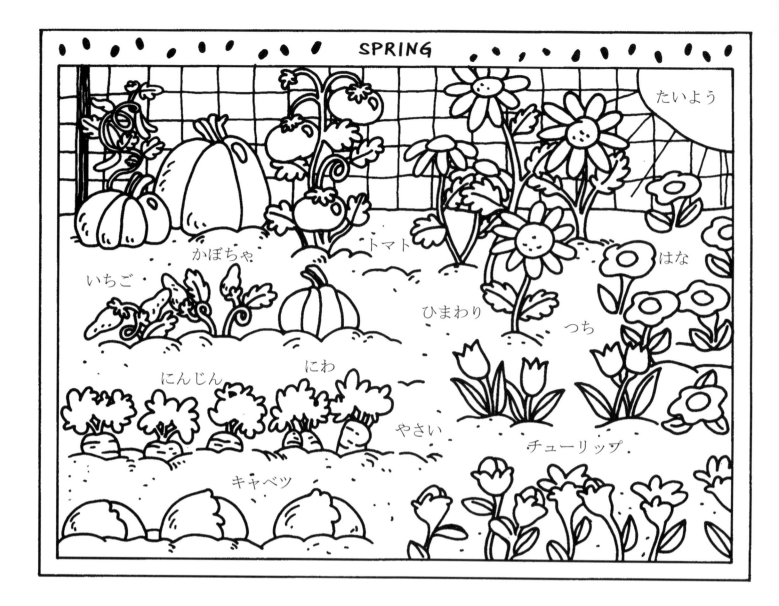

はる
Spring Vocabulary
Find the matching words in the picture.

soil _____   tulip _____

strawberries _____   carrots _____

vegetables _____   flowers _____

pumpkin _____   sunflower _____

cabbage _____   sun _____

tomato _____   garden _____

くも

ボート

サングラス

サンドイッチ

みずうみ

みずぎ

じきもの

シャツ

チーズ

かいがん

すいとう

カップ

バナナ

あり

すな

くつ

なつ
Summer Vocabulary
Find the matching words in the picture.

clouds _____

lake _____

beach _____

ant _____

sand _____

blanket _____

banana _____

sailboat _____

thermos _____

sunglasses _____

swimsuit _____

cheese _____

shoes _____

shirt _____

sandwich _____

cup _____

AUTUMN

あき
Autumn Vocabulary
Find the matching words in the picture.

sky _____

leaves _____

sweater _____

cat _____

skirt _____

nut _____

dog _____

jacket _____

basket _____

pants _____

tree _____

bird _____

WINTER

ふゆ
Winter Vocabulary
Find the matching words in the picture.

hill _____   ice skates _____

jacket _____   snow _____

ice _____   hat _____

snowflake _____   eyes _____

sled _____   carrot _____

hat _____   stick _____

coat _____   mitten _____

snowman _____   mouth _____

Answer Key (with Transliteration) for Vocabulary Words

はる haru (Spring)

	Translation	Transliteration		Translation	Transliteration
soil	つち	tsuchi	tulip	チューリップ	chûrippu
strawberries	いちご	ichigo	carrots	にんじん	ninjin
vegetables	やさい	yasai	flowers	はな	hana
pumpkin	かぼちゃ	kabocha	sunflower	ひまわり	himawari
cabbage	キャベツ	kyabetsu	sun	たいよう	taiyou
tomato	トマト	tomato	garden	にわ	niwa

なつ natsu (Summer)

	Translation	Transliteration		Translation	Transliteration
clouds	くも	kumo	thermos	すいとう	suitou
lake	みずうみ	mizuumi	sunglasses	サングラス	sangurasu
beach	かいがん	kaigan	swimsuit	みずぎ	mizugi
ant	あり	ari	cheese	チーズ	chîzu
sand	すな	suna	shoes	くつ	kutsu
blanket	しきもの	shikimono	shirt	シャツ	shatsu
banana	バナナ	banana	sandwich	サンドイッチ	sandoicchi
sailboat	ボート	bôto	cup	カップ	kappu

あき aki (Autumn)

	Translation	Transliteration		Translation	Transliteration
sky	そら	sora	dog	いぬ	inu
leaves	はっぱ	happa	jacket	ジャケット	jaketto
sweater	セーター	sêtâ	basket	かご	kago
cat	ねこ	neko	pants	ズボン	zubon
skirt	スカート	sukâto	tree	き	ki
nut	きのみ	kinomi	bird	とり	tori

ふゆ fuyu (Winter)

	Translation	Transliteration		Translation	Transliteration
hill	おか	oka	ice skates	アイススケート	aisusukêto
jacket	ジャケット	jacketto	snow	ゆき	yuki
ice	こおり	koori	hat	ぼうし	boushi
snowflake	ゆき	yuki	eyes	め	me
sled	そり	sori	carrot	にんじん	ninjin
hat	ぼうし	boushi	stick	えだ	eda
coat	うわぎ	uwagi	mitten	てぶくろ	tebukuro
snowman	ゆきだるま	yukidaruma	mouth	くち	kuchi